Dear **Cello Timer**,

Welcome to **Cello Time Scales**, where you'll find a lot more than just scales and arpeggios. There are plenty of fun pieces to play, puzzles to enjoy, and chances to make up your own tunes.

Each key has a fingering chart which shows you which finger pattern you'll need. Have a pencil ready to fill in the letter names of each scale, and remember to check the key signature in case any of the letters need a sharp ♯ or a flat ♭ sign after them. The dotted circles show that a finger is placed on the string but not played; you don't need to fill in these letter names.

The tinted circles on the chart are for the notes of the arpeggio. To help learn your arpeggios from memory, write down the arpeggio fingering like a telephone number in the space provided. Just write the fingering for going up and simply read it backwards to come down again. The letter names of the scale and arpeggio 'helpline' for D major are given to start you off.

Use the ideas below to play your scales and arpeggios in different ways. Keep practising and have fun!

Kathy and David Blackwell

Things to do with your scales and arpeggios

- Play them:
  1. With even notes and separate bows: 2. Slurred two notes to a bow:

- Play them with a long note on the key note or tonic:

- Dice game. Throw a dice and play one of the rhythms below on each note of the scale or arpeggio. Make up more rhythm patterns of your own. Football teams, your friends' names, and favourite foods can all be starting-points for your own rhythms.

- Find a friend and play your scales and arpeggios as rounds, like this:

D MAJOR one octave

Scale

Arpeggio

Arpeggio Helpline: Ring **0 3 0 4**

Rhythm game

Play each note of the scale and arpeggio with this rhythm:

Fid - dle   on   your   fin - ger   tips.

1. Finger tips

Try to keep your fingers down on the D string, and let your open A string ring out loud and clear!

Play 'Finger tips' with this rhythm variation:

Make up one of your own.

2. Low D, high D, A in between

Low D, high D, A in be-tween.

Low A, high A, low A a-gain.

Play the harmonics with a fast bow-stroke.

C MAJOR one octave

Scale

Arpeggio

Arpeggio Helpline: Ring _ _ _ _ _

Rhythm game

Play each note of the scale and arpeggio with this rhythm:

Jog - ging   quick - ly

4

3. Let's jog

Energetically

mf

cresc.   *f*

Try jogging with the metronome! Start in the slow lane with level 1 and work up to Olympic standard.

Level 1: steady ♩ = 60
Level 2: in training ♩ = 80
Level 3: Olympic standard ♩ = 100

4. Step, skip, jump!

Rea-dy, stea-dy, step,   and   rea-dy, stea-dy, skip,   and   rea-dy, stea-dy jump: it's

time   to   blast off!

*

Rea-dy, stea-dy, step,   and   rea-dy, stea-dy, skip,   and   rea-dy, stea-dy jump: it's

time   to   blast off!   Blast   off!

* Complete these four bars by using the G string notes in the same pattern as the first four bars.

G MAJOR one octave

Scale

Arpeggio

Arpeggio Helpline: Ring _ _ _ _

Rhythm game

Make up your own rhythm and play it on each note of the scale and arpeggio.
Write down your own rhythm here:

5. Follow me

I play first and then you'll fol-low me, ___ that's how we'll make har - mo - ny.

Hear the sound of this round, play to-ge-ther now and fol - low me.

Play this piece as a round, with an entry at the place marked *.

6. Arpeggio fanfare

Chorus

Verse

Copy or answer *

Copy or answer *

Chorus

* Make up a two-bar phrase using notes from the arpeggio of G major.
Create a new verse and take turns with your teacher to invent two-bar phrases to be copied or answered.

C MAJOR two octaves

Scale

Arpeggio

Arpeggio Helpline: Ring _ _ _ _ _ _ _

Rhythm game

Play each note of the scale and arpeggio with this rhythm:

Cus - tard   on   your   corn - flakes.

7. Fast food

8. What's in your sandwich?

Pea - nut but - ter, cheese, or ham; what shall we have to - day?

* (Make up your own filling.)

Pea - nut but - ter, cheese, or ham; what shall we have to - day?

* Think of a foody rhythm and play it on the notes of the C major arpeggio.

A NATURAL MINOR one octave

Scale

Arpeggio

Arpeggio Helpline: Ring _ _ _ _

Rhythm game

Play each note of the scale and arpeggio with this rhythm:

Play   a   folk   song.

9. French carol

15th century

Andante

mp

mf

p

10. Somerset folk song

Traditional

Lively

mf

f

mf

f

F MAJOR one octave

Scale

Arpeggio

Arpeggio Helpline: Ring _ _ _ _

Rhythm game

Play each note of the scale and arpeggio with this rhythm:

I   can   play   se - mi - qua - vers.

11. Accelerator

Be sure to start at a steady tempo.

12. Double decker

Be a composer

Make up your own piece using some easy double stopping.
Try playing your open strings together, perhaps trying to sound like Scottish bagpipes!

A MAJOR one octave

Scale

Arpeggio

Arpeggio Helpline: Ring _ _ _ _

Rhythm game

Play each note of the scale and arpeggio with this rhythm:

Flo - ri - da   State

13. Sweet Betsy from Pike

American

Be a composer

Find a rhythm that matches the words below and then write the answer in the empty box next to the word. The rhythms you need are scattered around the box. Remember that each part of the box is only worth one crotchet beat. Make up your own piece in A major using these American rhythms.

New York	
Maryland	
Pennsylvania	
New Jersey	

B♭ MAJOR one octave

Scale

Remember! This scale and arpeggio start with 2nd finger.

Arpeggio

Arpeggio Helpline: Ring _ _ _ _

Rhythm game

Play each note of the scale and arpeggio with this rhythm:

Two lit - tle an - gels.

14. Two little angels

Lively

Traditional
adapted

mf

Two lit - tle an - gels, all dressed in white, tried to play an E flat but it

would-n't go right; so they prac-tised and prac - tised all through the night, and

now they can play E flat and they make it sound right! So two lit-tle an-gels, ha-loes a-glow,

now they know just how to keep their 1st fin - ger low, now their B flats and E flats,

these sound al-right, those lit-tle an-gels play in tune now right through the night.

15. Knock, knock!

'Knock, knock.' 'Who's there?' 'An - drew.' 'An-drew who?'

*

'An - drew the cur - tains so I could - n't see if you were in!'

* Using notes from the key of B♭ major, write down an ending to this musical joke.

G MAJOR two octaves

Scale

Arpeggio

Arpeggio Helpline: Ring _ _ _ _ _ _ _

Rhythm game

Play each note of the scale and arpeggio with this rhythm:

Bon - jour, mes a - mis.

16. French folk song

Allegretto   Traditional

17. Eiffel Tower

Spend a jol - ly,   hap - py hour,   walk - ing up the   Eif - fel Tower!
jog - ging
run - ning

(Repeat*)

Climb down from the   high - est floor,   reach the ground then   say 'En - core!'
'En - core!'
'No more!'

* Try it a little faster on each repeat!

D HARMONIC MINOR one octave

Scale

Arpeggio

Arpeggio Helpline: Ring _ _ _ _

Rhythm game

Play each note of the scale and arpeggio with this rhythm:

Ju - pi - ter, Mars, and Ve - nus.

18. Theme from Mahler's First Symphony

19. Mission to Mars

Mysteriously

Rock-et on the launch-pad, let's take off. Wait-ing for the count-down,

now blast off! Speed-ing round the ga - la - xy on the way to Mars,

As - tro - nauts in rock - et ships, so - lar su - per - stars.

Be a composer

Compose your own space piece. Perhaps your piece could tell a story. Explore your cello for some special effects: harmonics, *glissandi*, or playing with the wood of the bow are a few to try. Or take the rhythm of some space words and make up a piece using notes from D harmonic minor. For example:

Shoot-ing star

C HARMONIC MINOR one octave

Scale

1 x 3

Arpeggio

Arpeggio Helpline:

Ring _ _ _ _ _

Rhythm game

Play each note of the scale and arpeggio with this rhythm:

C   min - or   is   the   key.

20. Old man of Peru

mf

There was an old man of Pe - ru, who dreamt he was eat-ing his shoe. He

L.H. pizz.

woke in the night in a ter - ri - ble fright! And found it was per-fect-ly true!

Crack the code!

Work out what this says! The number '1' means find the letter name of the first note in the scale of C minor, '2' means the second note, and so on. Write the correct letter in its box.

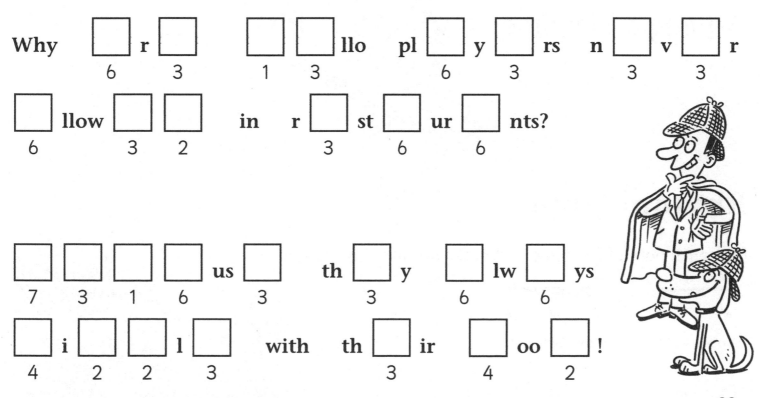

Why ☐r☐ ☐☐llo pl☐y☐rs n☐v☐r
     6 3   1 3   6 3   3 3

☐llow☐☐ in r☐st☐ur☐nts?
6   3 2   3   6   6

☐☐☐☐us☐ th☐y ☐lw☐ys
7 3 1 6   3   3   6   6

☐i☐☐l with th☐ir ☐oo☐!
4 2 2 3   3   4   2

G HARMONIC MINOR one octave

Scale

1 x 3

Arpeggio

Arpeggio Helpline: Ring _ _ _ _ _

Rhythm game

Play each note of the scale and arpeggio with this rhythm:

Spoo - ky   haun - ted house.

21. Haunted house

* Left-hand pizzicato.

You could try making up your own scary middle section for this piece. Try playing on the wrong side of the bridge for some really spooky sounds!

22. Le tambourin

Rameau

D MELODIC MINOR one octave

Scale

(Going up)

(Coming down)

Two notes change on the way down in the melodic minor scale—can you spot them?

Arpeggio

Look back to page 20 for the notes of the D minor arpeggio.

Rhythm game

Play each note of the scale and arpeggio with this rhythm:

I   like   the blues.

23. I gotta play those cello blues

24. Shalom Chaverim

Israeli

This is a minor-key round. It can be played in three parts with an entry at each of the places marked *.

C MELODIC MINOR one octave

Scale

(Going up)

(Coming down)

Two notes change on the way down in the melodic minor scale—can you spot them?

Arpeggio

Look back to page 22 for the notes of the C minor arpeggio.

Rhythm game

Make up your own rhythm and play it on each note of the scale and arpeggio.
Write down your own rhythm here:

25. Yellow cello

Down in the for-est there lives a big bear. He likes to

sit in his com-fy arm-chair. Play-ing his cel-lo that's

paint-ed bright yel-low, He sings, and growls, that cra-zy old bear!

* Try playing as a round, with the second part entering at *.

26. Escalator cha-cha

(up)

mf (down)   (up)

(down)   f

Fill in the missing notes. Add three crotchets to each incomplete bar. Use the ascending
G string notes from C melodic minor when the escalator is going 'up' and the descending
G string notes when the escalator is coming 'down'.

G MELODIC MINOR one octave

Scale

(Going up)

(Coming down)

Two notes change on the way down in the melodic minor scale—can you spot them?

Arpeggio

Look back to page 24 for the notes of the G minor arpeggio.

Rhythm game

Play each note of the scale and arpeggio with this rhythm:

F   sharp   or   F   nat - 'ral?

27. A bit of Bach

J. S. Bach (adapted)

28. Bump in the night

Creepily

I hear a sound, what can it be? Some-thing's out there!

Fine

Creep - ing a-bout, too dark to see, Oh what a scare!

D.C. al Fine

* gliss.

* What do you think is creeping about? Be a composer and invent some scary music of your own in these four bars. Try sliding your left hand up and down the string or tapping your instrument.

NATURAL MINORS one octave

G natural minor

D natural minor

Work out how to play the scale of C natural minor. Begin on the open C string and follow the same finger pattern as G and D natural minor.

Choose one of these natural minor scales and fill in the notes of your chosen scale on the chart to the right.

You'll find the notes for the minor arpeggios on the following pages: D minor p. 20, C minor p. 22, G minor p. 24.

29. Zum gali, gali

Lively

Traditional

* Make up a two-bar phrase using some of the notes from the scale of G natural minor. Create a new verse and take turns with your teacher to invent two-bar phrases to be copied or answered.

Music and text origination by Julia Bovee
Printed in England by Halstan & Co. Ltd, Amersham, Bucks.